COVID-19

Lockdown Nature Movies

A catalogue record of this book is available from the British Library.

First Edition: November 2021

ISBN: 978-1-84375-630-9

To order additional copies of this book please visit:
http://www.prestige-press.com/shirleyhughes

Published by: Prestige Press
Email: info@prestige-press.com
Web: http://www.prestige-press.com

Other Books by the author:

Persona
In Depth Of Soul
The Choices of Being
The Grass Isn't Always Greener
Rose Tinted Glasses
Leah's Journey
The Pink Flamingo Fellowship
Bilé
Academia
Pathway To The Unconscious
Sartre – In Focus
Mooloo
The Symbolic Mask
Ghostopia
Recognising The Soul
Transformation
Philosophy of Friendship
The Blue Bat Art Book

COVID-19

Lockdown Nature Movies

by

Dr. Shirley Hughes

Prestige Press

Contents

PART ONE

Lockdown

Chapter 1

Introduction

2020 will forever be known as the year of COVID-19, the Coronavirus Pandemic sweeping the world and where no-one is immune. Politically it will also be remembered as the year in which authoritarian regimes around the world made public their inadequacy, and for too many of us it will also be remembered as the year in which our own elected officials were too slow to act to prevent the loss of loved ones. Our societies too have been somewhat complacent and the effects of that complacency has been painful. Safety in this pandemic centres upon existentialist themes, such as each person's need to take responsibility for their own actions and choices in this crisis to keep both themselves and others safe from this disastrous pandemic which is ravaging our way of life and all aspects of it.

That is the first sense of the pandemic. The second sense which is more striking and more enduring stands for a decadence of culture which has led us into a currency-fixated complacency, especially with respect between humanity and nature. This complacency results in a lack of vigilance and a resulting inability to mount adequate defences against the outbreaks which ultimately tragically claim the lives of far too many citizens. However, all is not lost. We have united in the face of tragedy and many people have become better than they were before, setting aside narrow, selfish concerns to donate to hospitals, care for each other and stay home to avoid transmitting the virus.

Chapter 2

Lockdown

Living in lockdown need not be complicated, as much unhappiness is wrought from the burdens of our modern society. Most people even in this comparatively free country, through mere ignorance and mistakes, are so occupied with the fictitious cares and superfluously coarse labours of life, that the finer fruits cannot be plucked by them. There are many stresses which burden modern society. A large number of the population are under 'house arrest', so to speak. Confinement is broken only by the permitted exercise, for essential shopping, meaning food and medication, which gives us all more time than hitherto to reflect, and there is much to reflect on, not just the kind of philosophical questions that have preoccupied us over the years, but in what is going on in a world turned upside down. Keeping one's distance and wearing a mask is now pro social, whist proximity is anti social. It is an act of courtesy explicitly to cross the road to avoid someone. Careless talk costs lives, as pleasantries may be mixed with the ultimate unpleasantry of the invisible enemy, and sentences could be death sentences.

There is a strange convergence between altruism and self interest here, protecting ourselves. Avoiding going to work is mandatory if your work is not key. We play our part by staying home and hand washing. And so to hand washing. Our infinitely versatile hands on duty all our waking hours get everywhere. As the pathway carrying the heaviest traffic between our bodies and the material world, they are potentially super spreaders, incessantly touching surfaces touched by a hidden multitude of other hands. With these same hands we contact our own bodies and the food we prepare and the equipment that assists us to cook and eat. So there is much to think about, as we wash our hands and if we adhere to the prescribed duration and frequency of lavage, there is much time to do the thinking. The injunction to use two rounds of 'Happy Birthday' as a timer to ensure hand washing has been adequate as a starting point, and a startling reminder of the ingenuity of a species capable of re-purposing activities in such cunning ways. What is being in lockdown and isolation doing for us? It teaches us to treasure the moments of happiness and joy we share, just because humanity is painfully inadequately equipped to cope with stresses and stimuli it encounters.

The passing of time dulls our attention to detail and despite the power of our civilisation the mass of humanity remains slow to respond to threats from this virus. The quintessence of existence for us reacting to the current pandemic is that individuals die when the collective fails to recognise or respond adequately to foreseeable threats. As predicted, the pandemic is far from over, and may never be. Yet it is no more right to say we deserve our fate than it is correct to assume that one day the mass of humanity will be able to respond to all threats to it without loss of life, insofar as we continue to live unawares in the midst of this conflict between our species and nature, and life and death will continue to be dictated by means beyond our control, and even our understanding. We can only hope and love and act and be as good as we can be to attain that stillness and peacefulness of mind and body as in lockdown, leaving chaotic living behind when we emerge.

Chapter 3

The Real Disease

What is the real disease? It is the tendency to bring about death by action or inaction. Some people do not know they have it, the monster lurking within. Others have learned to live with it. The person who has the fewer lapses of attention keeping that endless watch upon himself lest in the careless moment he should breathe in someone's face and fasten the virus upon him.

The absurd nature of suffering and the human condition at large ultimately seems to be the way in which people are used up by the rest of humanity. There was a politically led desire to avoid a false alarm at the outset of the virus, even though it became obvious enough to the experts what the increasing death toll was, but yet things did not become quite pressing enough to call the politicians to action to prevent things from spiralling out of control.

The victims ... there is a sense in which the pandemic is in fact a cure, for although it kills too many and causes too much grief, it also breaks down the immoral conditions in which we lived before it struck. It brings solidarity, community and meaning back into focus in our lives. It finally holds the politicians to account. The reluctance with which the precautionary measures were taken up is woefully indicative of the inadequacy of the machinery of the state to act upon the basis of unfamiliar evidence to bring into effect measures which might even have prevented the outbreak. Therefore it has been necessary that the virus strikes to establish itself among us before anything is done about it, and terrible that there was not more readiness upon the part of the government to act upon the early warning signs recognised by the experts.

Chapter 4

Social Isolation

Experiencing social isolation, so what might philosophy have to say about social distancing and for some, social isolation? Social distancing in complete solitude becomes a one-off social experiment, a unique utopian account of simple living, a journey of spiritual discovery and a manual of self-reliance, which is perhaps overly idealistic. The thing is, finding serenity in privacy and isolation becomes a compelling aspect of the experience, so how could anybody begin to be isolated? The answer is to turn inward whilst isolating, and you will not feel lonely. Loneliness is a creation of our own misinformed mental diversions. A kind of comforting perspective on loneliness is that no matter how hard we try, there will always be a chasm of consciousness between ourselves and others.

What sort of space is that which separates one person from another and makes him solitary? No exertion of the legs can bring two minds much nearer to one another, so we had best get acquainted with what is reachable, and that is ourselves. We are our own best friends. We should reframe our negative thoughts into positive and productive ones. We can reframe the crippling emotion of loneliness into self-fulfilling solitude. Another tool of the mind is that stoicism we have within ourselves to let the world, negative or positive, wash over us without affecting us, to observe the world as if having an out-of-body experience. By a conscious effort of the mind we can stand aloof from actions and their consequences, and all things good and bad go by us like a torrent. In this way we are able to overcome the pull of loneliness whilst in isolation. Live deliberately. See if you can deliberately live a fulfilling life with the bare essentials and shedding the unnecessary surplus of modern life.

How to live deliberately may be a little bit more difficult to reframe negative thoughts and let the world rush past us without affecting us. By a conscious effort of the mind we can do this. It may be difficult to make sense of what is happening around us. For some during this crisis the anxiety and fear has become palpable. Before we can understand the world we must first understand ourselves. This is what we need to achieve. While many sit at home trying to figure out what to do, instead of looking out there to the world to extinguish our boredom, turn inward and know yourself. Most times when you understand yourself and truly come to know who you are, what you think or why you like what you like, thinking can be an impetus to starting anew. So rather than lamenting, take a breath of fresh air instead and reflect happily on your life and what you have to do. Normalcy will come back, so be happy and let yourself be optimistic.

Chapter 5

Transcendentalism

Like existentialism, transcendentalism was never systemised into a formal school of thought. Some of its concepts remain amorphous but unlike existentialism, it propounded a somewhat naïve optimism towards humanity. Transcendentalism's philosophical influence on other thinking is latent, if under appreciated. So what can a 19th century philosophy such as transcendentalism offer us in our present challenging time amidst a pandemic? We are, as it were, living a unique experiment in isolation, trying to live a deliberate and fulfilling life with basic essentials and shedding the unnecessary surplus of our modern existence, so starting our reflective life. It could be said that it describes an application of transcendentalist philosophy by showing how to live deliberately and how to be alone with ourselves, how to embrace solitude without feeling lonely away from other people. Solitude we find is good and is very different from loneliness.

During these unusual times we must turn inward, so we can understand outward to be introspective. Transcendentalism is an intellectual movement intent on positivity, re-thinking contemporary society, transforming culture from unreflective conformity to a purified individualism. Transcendentalism's modus operandi was always intuition, not reason, and also an early form of critical theory, a rationalist critique of contemporary society rooted in individual progress. Transcendentalists are known for their overflowing optimism, whether practical or not. They say they love to be alone, as they have never found a companion so companionable as solitude, and are for the most part more lonely when amongst people than when they stay at home thinking about the simple things in life and what makes them truly happy. That helps them get through self isolation.

How can we transform isolation into a positive solitude? So let us be real here. All this transcendentalism guru talk is easier said than done and there is no distinct line distinguishing loneliness from solitude. It is a blurred spectrum which we can find ourselves drifting along back and forth. Some have never felt lonesome or in the least oppressed by a sense of solitude and it is possible to love solitude if we understand correctly that being an introvert can be more exciting then being an extrovert. Doing a project all on our own is one way solitude can have a beneficial effect on our mental health. We can transform feelings of loneliness into fulfilling solitude when we engage with ourselves in projects we value. Shedding the things in our modern life that stress us out and simplifying our lives is what helps. It is not things as such that stresses us out. It is stress itself that stresses us out.

Chapter 6

Conclusion to Part One

Since the months of lockdown the days seem to have followed each other at an accelerated pace. Time speeds up until the sequence of days and nights looks like a stroboscopic flickering. Either way, there has been plenty of time for philosophical and less philosophical brooding on the unfolding catastrophe that goes under the name COVID-19. We have witnessed heroism and kindness, altruism and patient, attentive care. Neighbours have discovered neighbourliness, citizens have embraced civic values, individuals facing unemployment, even destitution, have taken it upon themselves to worry about the needs of vulnerable strangers. But the pandemic has also cast light on something far less attractive, in particular our political class and the social order over which it governs.

The COVID-19 story in the UK has been dire. Due to the dithering and incompetence of the government in the run-up to lockdown, the mortality rate per capita in the UK is at the time of writing the highest in the world. The economic hit to the UK is likely to be world beating and this despite Britain's good fortune in being relatively late to experience the pandemic, and therefore having been given time to prepare and learn from experience elsewhere. Some may be surprised that a nation with the reputation for competence and governance and other such virtues should have failed so disastrously with the challenge presented by the virus. Then too, there was the lack of personal protective equipment for health care staff and others in various front lines, an abysmal and continuing failure to develop track and trace to isolate cases, and the many COVID-19 related deaths in care homes. The pandemic has exacerbated pre-existing inequalities and iniquities. It is clear that fundamental change is needed. Such change secured through radical fiscal policies that address not only economic inequality will require a different kind of politician.

For politicians who have a moral compass, vision and competence to ascend to power requires a transformation of the conversation citizens have with each other. This must mean something profoundly different from the disconnected, reactive, narrow minded, mean spirited, ill informed and lie strewn discourse orchestrated by media platforms owned by, and therefore in the interests of, billionaires. Coming to philosophy. What can philosophy bring to the conversation we must have if our post pandemic world is to be better than the world that was ambushed by COVID-19? The most obvious philosophical source of contribution to the much needed conversation is political philosophy. There is serious work to be done and philosophy will make its contribution to a better world for us all to instigate the changes required for the betterment of every one of us. Philosophical and collective conversation is the vital ingredient replacing mind with matter in shaping events. It is much needed. Philosophers have always interpretated the world in various ways and it will now help to change it in the pursuit of its ultimate end.

PART TWO

NATURE

Chapter 1

Introduction

Being outside in nature, especially at this time in lockdown, is an almost poignant experience, as we are all aware that we cannot venture out to places in nature now shut to us. We should in time be able to return to the kind of nature that makes us gasp, as in standing on a snow-covered windy peak taking in the utter vastness of the landscape and momentarily forgetting ourselves and realising our own finitude. Our gardens become the refuge of enlightenment in particular for a couple able to share the experience. Being outside in nature, albeit in our gardens, needs a contemplative distance that allows us to linger to immerse ourselves and thereby to lose ourselves, to think and reflect.

We can now reunite beauty with sublimity, so we are freed from self centredness, so saving ourselves from the grip of consumerism. It contributes towards making our lives meaningful and is what makes us feel that life is worth living. Meaningfulness is about connecting to oneself. In nature we can find purpose wherein life becomes valuable connecting to something grander. Today the domain of actual human freedom is a tiny circumscribed plot of land and we recognise that and appreciate it and nurture it in perhaps a new way to how we experienced it before lockdown.

Chapter 2

Shared Experience

However beautiful the experience in nature can be, when alone it is the lack of companionship that can transform an otherwise beautiful experience into a depressive one. As we travel through life we learn more about ourselves and who we are. These insights come to us in bursts as we enjoy and cope with life's highs and lows, but such understanding does not exist in a relational vacuum. Being alone can make us realise a need for a shared experience. We understand ourselves in part by recognising how we are similar to and yet different from others. However, some people are perfectly fine on their own, while others need company to accentuate an event or perhaps to even enjoy it at all. Is this just a difference of character traits among people, or is one disposition better than the other? At first sight it would appear that an ability to be satisfied with one's own experience is quite an existential handicap.

Recent psychological research suggests that shared experiences are amplified, both the good and the bad, but such research is narrow in scope and differences in types of experience as well as individual differences in the magnitude of amplification. Can such variances be significant enough to be pathological or is there something wrong with me? We are a species inherently social. We seem to have our own desire for interaction and sense of belonging. It is not the yearning for inclusiveness but rather the character of shared versus solitary experience and why experiences for some are not good enough on their own. The meaning of life resides with our shared experiences. Our loved one is the object of our affection as well as our partner on life's journey. In a certain sense a life fully lived is in part lived through that significant other. This is what we are left with if we reject an appeal to a higher power to give our lives meaning, but perhaps it might be overstating the case if there is a wide range of psychological disposition towards shared experience. There is a broad spectrum of experiences that people find valuable and which give life meaning, as being in our own garden together in lockdown appreciating the nature around us is to us a valuable experience. Clearly not all valuable experiences need to be shared, although many by their very nature do. But irrespective of what we value, the experience gets amplified if it is shared, albeit at different intensities. As such, sharing experiences makes them more significant and makes them more meaningful. Nevertheless the sharing of experience is not only about amplification.

Many of our most valuable moments are special precisely because they are shared experiences, as they assume their significance in the act of sharing. This also highlights that it is not sufficient for an event to be shared with just anyone to make it significant. Who we share it with can be central to its meaning. So what is so great about shared experiences? Besides being some of our most memorable moments, and also amplifying our experiences, a shared experience has the virtue that it continues to be shared. Sharing allows the experience to be relived more vividly through mutual recollection and conversations. It affirms the reality of the experience and the character of it, its sweetness is validated by the other's similar perception. The lasting impression is the more vivid by having a loved one there. Shared experience need not only be viewed in terms of circumscribed moments in time, but may also be viewed more broadly. Together with that someone special who accompanies us through life, there is a sense of it being more than one alone bearing witness to our existence. By sharing our experience there is someone other than ourselves who is aware of the sum total of our journey.

This temporal dimension of shared experience also has the virtue of being one of the few ways we can become immortal, because a shared experience does not belong to us alone. It has the quality of living on once we re gone. By living on in the memory of those we leave behind, we do not get a new lease of life, but in a certain sense the lease of life we have had gets extended. So is there something wrong with us? Clearly being dependent on others to heighten our experience makes them more meaningful and makes us more psychologically vulnerable. Our state of mind is not within our sole control, but contingent on being accompanied.

There are ways of mitigating vulnerability, for example meditation techniques can allow us to find contentment in our own head space. Finding peace of mind in solitude can help us to be less exposed to the contingencies in life, particularly at this time in lockdown and self isolation, but such solitary solace surely cannot itself be what fundamentally brings our life meaning. If our lives have meaning, it resides with us, but not necessarily as isolated islands of self contentment. Our most memorable moments are shared, but it might also be the meaning of life. It is for us combining and sharing life with our loved one during lockdown during this pandemic, staying safe at home in our own garden revering nature enhancing the experience, one we will never forget.

Chapter 3

Seeing True Nature

These days we would all be hard pushed to find a corner of the biosphere unaltered by human hands. In a lot of places nature has been rendered almost incapable of sustaining healthy life. Humanity needs to explain and explore environmental thought. Our society has caused a loss of species estimated to be a thousand more times rapid than the rate of extinction that would have occurred by the absence of human activity. So extensive is the human impact on nature that signifies irreversible changes in nature's ecosystems. How did we get here and how is it we are able to carry on unleashing ever more devastating effects on the wonders of our natural environment and all living entities? We need to come to a better understanding of nature and in so doing we may also see ourselves as we really are.

Disharmony is both a symptom and a cause of alienation from the natural world, as well as blindness to our true nature. Reversing this process means breaking down artificial boundaries between humanity and nature to reveal the underlying unity and wholeness. Both philosophically and ecologically personal interests can be seen as the interests of the whole. This realisation can set the tone for a better balance between society and nature. Lockdown has enabled us to recognise how important nature, our gardens and the wild spaces are and why we all need to respect, care for and nurture it. The future of our planet and regard to our natural environment for the fist time is at least partly under the control of conscious, reasoning human beings, but for any kind of a viable shared future, humanity must nurture an awareness and understanding that enables the regulation of our impulses and behaviour. This is a morality based on self discipline. People must cultivate a new appreciation and reverence for the inviolate sanctity and compassion of nature as a basis for every decision, as well as assessing the appropriateness of every action to protect, save and expand our green spaces to prevent environmental destruction; which in some cases seems to be an outer manifestation of inner affliction.

We have to treat people and the natural environment as inseparable. The way we perceive and understand ourselves is critical in determining how we act. It shapes the way we perceive and understand each other and the natural environment. Environmental destruction therefore is inevitable; if our thoughts are polluted then our actions will be polluted too and so will the consequences. We need to see things differently. The first ethical precept is that of non harm to our natural environment and the first rule is to advocate conservation measures for all wildlife to give direct guidance on the proper attitude towards the natural world.

Chapter 4

A Perfect World

A visual environment that is meaningful is beautiful for personal and sentimental reasons. It seems that a deep part of human nature feels most a peace in a particular natural environment, one with greenery, with open areas punctuated by trees, with water and wildlife. That's the habitat our species evolved in and it has extended itself into our brain. It may be that there is an eco paradise that may be the kind of environment in which our species feels happiest and that people use to symbolise the ideal world, ie the Garden of Eden. Many people collapse the rarefied notion of the perfect world into some super saturated essence, and look for a graphic way to describe that essence, such as a landscape of favourite things or an eclectically assembled perfect world. There are several recurring themes, peace, harmony, more nature and a stabilised environment, leaving behind all kinds of authoritarianism and the dire problems we have today.

Asking people what their notion of a perfect world in nature is would involve a simple truism. Any image of a heartfelt desire remembered or rehearsed exerts a dynamic but stealth-like form which wants to carry reality into being. If a more or less perfect world of nature is possible at all, we can only imagine that it would emerge slowly over time. The purpose of being in nature is simply to show how personal happiness can be achieved, not by trying to create a utopia, nor by reorganising a person's knowledge and beliefs, a relatively simple and self sufficient life described as a kind of pleasure, a pleasurable life free from life's physical pain and much more importantly, free from anxiety and mental turmoil. A wise person would be careful and prudent who maintained a life of calm simplicity. The ultimate goal philosophically is ataraxia which is peace of mind and tranquillity characteristic of a life which perceives no serious problems. Ataraxia requires above all the removal of disturbing fears found in most people and in most cultures. Nature's perfect world is the salvation of mankind. We find positive values of the uncultivated wild too. Life of material ease can be substituted by the need for nature to provide aesthetic and spiritual value for our soul.

Chapter 5

Environmental Philosophers

There is a conspicuous lack of environmental philosophers. If our natural environmental problems are at their root, not just scientific or technical in nature, but a problem of human attitudes, beliefs and values, the philosophers are probably among the best equipped to bring light rather than heat to discussions. It means public input not intramural arguments in academic philosophy journals and symposia. The problem is not lack of talent. There are excellent environmental philosophers out there, or rather in there, because we rarely encounter their work outside of their ivory towers. Environmental philosophy books are virtually completely absent in book stores. Even the typical New Age book stores, which often have sections devoted to nature or environment rarely carry books by academic environmental philosophers.

There is obviously a market for philosophy books on the environment. This state of affairs suggests that either the people who otherwise consume philosophy are not very interested in the philosophical treatment of environmental issues, or that people who are interested in environmental issues do not believe that, or are not aware that, philosophers have anything to contribute. Or both. In policy discussions, environmental agencies desperately need the kind of conceptual and normative analysis that philosophers can provide. If philosophy is devoted to confronting life's most profound questions including how to live, then our current environmental predicament is a philosophical problem par excellence.

It ought to be getting a lot of attention from the philosophically inclined. Environmental issues are pressing. Human activity is putting such a strain on the natural functions of the earth that the planet's ecosystems to sustain future generations can be no longer taken for granted. A real problem exists and it is worthy of serious philosophical attention. It is a real, earthly problem of epic proportions, not a stimulating intellectual exercise. Philosophy, it is said, deals with timeless questions, but we may not have much time to ensure a stable, hospitable planet like the one we have had for the last 10,000 years. Right now the possibility that we are destroying the planet would seem to be a pretty important philosophical subject matter. The problem I suspect stems from a view of philosophy that still largely predominates, which is that it consists of expanding the mind, and is to be studied for the sake of the questions themselves to enrich our intellectual imagination.

Are the pragmatics of figuring out how to live sustainably on the earth actually too down-to-earth for fans of contemplative philosophical traditions? Maybe it is time to prioritise. Abstract philosophical problems, whilst universal in scope, are not pressing, but our environmental problems which cry out for philosophical treatment are. Our environmental predicament affects every human being and every living thing on our planet. Philosophy has never been in a hurry. It is not used to pressure, but that is because despite a valuable tradition of challenging the taken-for-granted, it has always taken for granted a healthy, stable planet. But it is a new world now where timeless questions may have a time limit. At this moment in history we need more philosophers applying their insight and expertise to environmental issues, and we need their input in the public arena. Environmental philosophy is a discipline whose time is now.

Chapter 6

Conclusion to Part Two

We have needed our gardens and outside spaces more now in lockdown. They have been for us at this time nature's perfect world. In these safe havens of smells, colours, textures, wildlife noises, weather changes, heightened senses, seeing small details of nature, new experiences, awareness of silence and becoming immersed and absorbed by just being there. It is something priceless, something we respect and nurture and cultivate. It is vital for our wellbeing and mental health. Our gardens have given us experiences, bringing us closer together, and we are seeing true nature for real and up close. And we spend valuable time out in them. For many of us they have become a Garden of Eden. Each one is our landscape to aesthetically assemble as we want and it is an environment we can control and be free in mind and spirit. It is our salvation in such a strange, weird new world of lockdown. It also brings the importance of environmental philosophy to the fore. We need our greenery and all that the natural environment offers us.

Once lockdown eases and we can again return to visiting our natural environments, the great vistas, countryside, parks and wildlife centres and the like, will our experiences be tempered by social distancing still in place and being aware of other people out too? Lockdown may seem to be the safest, wisest place to be in our own gardens, sheltering in seclusion and appreciating our own nature, whilst being able to contemplate the wider natural world and the great sadness of its destruction. Reverence and conservation is vital and natural places need to be cherished and expanded and taken care of by every one of us. This is nature's perfect environment we are all a part of. Lockdown has made us recognise this while keeping us safe. Now we need to keep our natural environment safe.

Note: We do not need an atom bomb at all; the uprooting of human beings is already taking place. It is no longer an earth on which human beings live today.

Online we feel separated from reality, the causal efficacy of our perceptions having been shoved further away from us. Nature is once again bifurcated illegitimately, into the natural world and the human world. But we are nature. To deny we exist in a natural world as entirely natural beings is to deny we are human. The online world, whilst a temporary saviour in the current crisis, runs the risk of becoming a permanent curse. Knowledge gained through the online world is cold and hollow. Before COVID-19 the world we inhabited was a world we perceived and understood through our own conceptualisation. Now the world we inhabit only serves to remove us further from our nature, from the natural, from humanity. Perception is everything when it comes to our knowledge of the world. A world perceived online is one which can only serve to make people less human.

PART 3

MOVIES

Chapter 1

Introduction

In these days of lockdown we have been given time to enjoy the pleasures of life, and for some of us viewing movies has been a special activity. In my vast collection, particular movies stand out for their philosophical aspects, probably not obvious to those unfamiliar with philosophy, but as a philosopher a great discovery to me personally, so much so that I have chosen movies that lend themselves to philosophical issues and themes within their construction. Movie makers over decades have made great movies and many are filmic expositions of the deepest ethical questions that have been posed by philosophers. In such movies the aspect of philosophy is never articulated explicitly, and certainly not intentionally, but when philosophers view such movies, philosophical aspects reveal themselves and precipitate discussion and thoughts, which enhances and enriches the viewing experience for the philosopher in particular.

These movies might imply that the subject matter is about epistemology, how we understand the world, or about metaphysics, the nature of reality or between conflicts of consequentialist ethics and their deontological counterpart. Movie makers are also not usually associated with metaethics, the comparison of ethical theories and not particularly known for deep knowledge of the finer points of moral philosophy or any other philosophy. Without realising, movie makers sometimes use their movies to teach us moral lessons. The theme in some movies is people's inability to work together to solve serious problems, or tragedy about how a lack of communication causes chaos and collapse in societies. They show a point which no sane person could fail to be depressed by, the capacity of the human race to ignore problems like climate change and problems serious enough to threaten civilisation. As a species, we may be irrational in ignoring these problems but we are also irrational in understanding ways that climate change does not happen all at once.

The danger it poses creeps up on us at an imperceptible, slow rate. It takes some scientific understanding to grasp the models used to predict its effects and there are vested interests that stand to make money by encouraging inertia and lack of action, and inertia is easy to encourage among people who already have a lot on their minds. None of these points would apply however in movies where people are killing people. The problem would be immediately apparent, its effects obvious and the problems are obvious too: shoot before anyone shoots you. These conflicts to the philosopher viewer are a battle between utilitarian ethics, which assume that the end justifies the means, and the deontological belief that we must always represent the rights of the individual. As far as movies go, the most recognisable form of utilitarianism is often associated with the greatest happiness principle, this being the idea that the right action in any situation of moral choice is the one that creates or enables the greatest happiness of the greatest number of people in the participating audiences.

Movie makers of course do not answer to the philosophical or recognise it even, as their concerns are for a gripping story performed brilliantly by actors at the height of their powers, which also have a dazzling cast of aspiring would-be actors too on the cusp of superstardom. Many movies nowadays showcase underlying philosophical ideas within their themes, whether movie makers are aware of that or not. It enables philosophers to engage in movies intellectually as well as enjoying the movies themselves. The moral within a movie is that it is very hard to shed light on the human condition, otherwise the results could simply be a slow plodding and irrelevant movie. The most acclaimed and popular movies seem to be those with moral allegories, in which more characters function as catalysts, forcing surviving humans into improvised communities whose continued existence depends on ethical adaptation. These microcosms of humanity offer movie makers the opportunity to examine how people respond when their perceptions of the basic rules of the world change, and to critique how they make decisions based upon these new rules. In an apocalyptic landscape people can no longer rely on making decisions based on dogmatic assumptions. Those are luxuries of civilisation.

Failure to join the fight against an invading apocalypse would be just stupid. Some movies for example import a message by telling a story that although it may be possibly possessing supernatural elements is recognisably like a real situation. Setting their movies in an unreal scene, these movies create a critical distance between the audience and situations. If all goes well, the movie will cause people to see something about the way the characters behave, that short sightedness can lead to tragic results and then realise and notice that real people behave in the same way. There would be several models for ethical decision making in which to choose most involved assessments of the problems, gathering all the information to identify potential courses of action and then evaluating the likely consequences of these actions.

The principles are autonomy, non maleficence, beneficence, justice and fidelity. Simply stated, people should respect independence and individual choice, avoid harming each other, help when they can, treat others fairly and forge loyalties. These can only be put into action once communication within communities has formed, and in the tradition of movies characters focus on their own personal survival or gain, which usually leads to that character's downfall. In effect in movies which show a message, if people look closely they will recognise themselves in it. However, if a movie is to impart a message the circumstances facing its characters must resemble those faced by real people to be authentic. Although the premise of some moves may be far fetched, the ideas behind them are not usually. Environmental decay, war, destruction, are all realities in our rapidly changing society. Navigating this hostile world requires leadership and we need to question its values as well as our own processes of decision making. If we do not ethically consider all the options, then we are on a path of self destruction as depicted in some movies. We love the movies and our enjoyment as philosophers is emphasised by having the ability to see beyond the obvious portrayed and to venture into the mind of the movie makers, engage with the characters and content presented. In this we escape from the everyday into another dimension, an exciting and stimulating adventure. Life would not be the same without movies to watch. We love them.

Chapter 2

Melancholia

Lars von Trier's movie Melancholia could be interpreted as a logical consequence of the history of European nihilism, whose most significant proponents were philosophers. In the movie the Danish director seems to be constructing an argument which not only questions the value of life, but also invites us to change our status from mortals to moribund beings. The planet Melancholia is on a collision course with Earth. This movie's terrifying apocalypse is completely original, focusing not on the biological or physical destruction of our planet and species. Instead it emphasises the psychological distress of two particular Earth dwellers, two sisters, one of whom is mentally ill, being severely melancholic. Melancholia's introduction is a depiction of the planetary dance of death combined with an ironic introduction to the history of art.

The introduction is shot in slow motion and the accompanying music symbolises the astronomical and the astrological clash of two planets. It could be seen as an abstract of Melancholia summarising the whole move. If the alliance between love and death and the subsequent destruction of the principle of love are the atmospheric message of the introduction, the nihilistic motto of the whole movie would be that the Earth is evil. We do not need to grieve for it. This attitude is reminiscent of Gnosticism. Its first principle was that the world of matter, the Earth, is evil, and that humankind is the damaged creation of an evil divine power. The nihilism proposed in the 20th century by various writers draws the similarly disturbing conclusion that because of our inherent defects, human beings must be destroyed; adapting one of the noble truths of Buddhism, that suffering must be annihilated by Nirvana. Lars von Trier illustrates a similar destructiveness in Melancholia in depicting the 'dark night of the soul' and as we see in the movie, the personalised 'dark night of the soul' may be even more significant than the 'dark night of the world'; the relationship of the two sisters , one having a controlling attitude, with the other having severe melancholia.

The sisters give the suggestion of a sadomasochistic couple, or of the feedback dynamics between a psychiatrist and reluctant patient, and it is interesting that at the end of the movie this relationship is reversed, with the collision of the planets imminent, the stoic philosopher's creed might be, 'though the world perishes let there be knowledge'. The end of the movie sees the two sisters facing the apocalypse. The controlling sister breaks down completely, while her melancholic sister keeps calm, suggesting the theory that mentally ill people face external catastrophes more easily, because they are more accustomed to traumas and intense psychological imbalances. This could make intelligible the idea hinted at in the movie, that the nihilistic night when one inwardly dies, descends into hell and cannot imagine a return from the inferno when our entire world dies inside us, is even more scarier than the night of the sense of cosmic death. This thesis would be absurd if considered from a rationalistic perspective.

How could the spiritual death of one individual count for more than the demise of mankind? Lars von Trier's vision of apocalypse in Melancholia puts it in the same category of romantic nihilism, which starts from the psychological disintegration of the individual and moves out to a project of universal destruction. First one of us dies on the inside and then all must follow, this is the incontrovertible rule of nihilistic violence. In the imaginary universe, the melancholia lives are transformed into an ode to death. For instance there is a scene when the mentally ill sister gives herself to the planet of death, worshipping it naked as Melancholia menacingly approaches. What could Melancholia suggest? Perhaps the director is expressing our deepest unconscious desire to be absolved of existence, as he is expressing the mysterious will to die, and the instinct of death which has its roots in the care of our civilisation. If love and death collide, we must hang on to our capacity for love until it transforms the power of death.

Chapter 3

Inception

The plot of the movie Inception involves the characters entering into a corporate executive's dream to implant an idea into his mind. For the idea to work, the dreamer must not realise that the idea has been implanted, so they construct a three-layered dream within a dream within a dream, in which they can disguise themselves as projections of the dreamer's psyche. A subplot of the movie is that the main character's parents and his wife got so stuck deep inside layers of the dream world that they grew old in their dream life. To escape he had to convince his wife that they were not in reality, but when she awoke with that idea still in her mind, she thought she was still dreaming, and to escape she killed herself. A philosophically interesting subtext concerns the metaphysical status of the character throughout the movie, where the whole movie itself is an elaborate dream of his. At the end we are deliberately left unsure what is the case.

Have you ever been sure that you have awoken from a dream, to find out you are actually still sleeping? Philosophers wanted to establish what is possible beyond doubt about whether we can ever tell for certain if we are dreaming or not. In fact our minds could be confused by various deceptions. Philosophers consider the possibility that we are being totally deceived in dreaming. This is where the radical scepticism comes into play, for if we cannot even tell for sure whether we are dreaming, then how can we know for certain any truth about the world in which we seem to live? Then we realise that even if we were mistaken about everything, then we must be thinking, for one cannot ever be deceived unless one is thinking and knowing for sure that one thinks, then it must follow that one exists, there must be a thinking thing. This is where the famous statement 'I think, therefore I am' comes from, because whatever can or cannot be knowing, this is at least beyond doubt. The philosopher's solution to the problem of dreaming versus reality is to argue that our memory can never connect our dreams with each other, and with the course of life in the way, it is in the habit of dealing with events that occur when we are awake. This is a way to distinguish dreams from reality and so can provide a basis for holding that you are not currently dreaming.

On the contrary, the premise behind some of the action in Inception is ultimately a rejection of the philosopher's solution to the dream argument. Even when the character is dreaming in the movie, he is fully awake to the possibility that he might be dreaming. So in the movie it is impossible to tell whether you are dreaming or not, albeit in many dreams within the movie we see things like the impossible staircase, which makes turns as it ascends or descends yet forms a continuous loop, so that a person could climb forever and ever and never get anywhere. Yet philosophers tell us we cannot dream what we have not experienced. That is why in the movie the dreamers who created the worlds and levels of the dreams are always using pieces of places that are familiar to them.

Philosophically speaking we cannot create anything absolutely new in our thoughts, only combine experiences and ideas which are already known to us. The only thing we know for sure in the state of doubt is our own thoughts. In the context of the movie, inception means an idea planted in someone's mind without their knowledge of this happening, and the character explains that this is only possible if the subject is in a deep enough sleep. Then the person can truly believe it was their own thoughts created by themselves whilst they were dreaming. Thus while in a dream state, things can be suggested to us by people who have invaded our dream world, in which the idea suggested seems plausible to us, and we may even remember the dream incident at a later point, believing it was our own thought, which is the premise of the movie. We hear this explained in Inception when the character tells us that he used inception on his wife. In Inception, in a dream, time is slower, days can pass there in what amounts to only a few minutes or an hour in the conscious world. So can the control central to the idea of Inception really happen? Can an idea really happen? Can an idea really be planted into minds of others whilst they are sleeping? While we are awake we can have an idea implanted. We can be influenced to make certain decisions and we can be persuaded to think or act in a certain way. If this can be done while we are awake, why not sleeping too?

The concept is entirely possible, may not be the way the movie shows it, but possible nonetheless. The questions remains, what distinguishes dreams from reality? This question is precisely why the movie Inception ends in doubt over whether the character is still dreaming or awake, by supposing we can think we are dreaming, whether or not we are. Inception makes dreams nearly indistinguishable from reality. However the movie's protagonists have real world objects called totems which have weights or other properties known only to their owners. They use them so they cannot be deceived about being in a dream by someone else. Only in the real world will a totem fall the way it is supposed to, and its owner can tell if they are in a dream state or reality. We are left seeing the totem spinning on a table when the movie cuts to the credits, leaving us not knowing or being able to tell whether the character was dreaming, since the original time when he created his totem and defined its behaviour might itself have been in a dream. This ending is perfect, as we are still searching for the answer to this question.

Chapter 4

L'Avenir (Things to Come)

Hanson-Love's movie L'Avenir manages to deliver a searing indictment of the state of Western philosophy and is an exceptionally understated movie. At the start of the movie a middle aged female professor of philosophy is haunted by a vague malaise while seemingly having no insight into its cause. She tries to get through a picket line of her demonstrating students to get into the Paris university where she works. When students later interrogate her apparent lack of concern she retorts that she is not here to talk politics but to teach. In the classroom, indifference to political issues from her is so thorough that not only does she have no opinion on the strike's objectives, but she discourages her students from critically engaging in the matter. Instead she proceeds to read an obscure text by a little known philosopher raising a completely abstract question for her students to ponder.

Later on a former student of hers seeks her out to tell her how grateful he is for her inspirational mentoring, which has transformed his life. She has made no genuine commitments to anyone or any cause and because of that she can hold on to nothing of her own. As her life unfolds we discern that she is not truly reconciled to any decision she takes, nor to any relationship or role she plays. She lacks the courage of conviction. Even when her husband announces that he is leaving her for another woman, she does not entertain the possibility of sacrificing her pride to try and keep him in her life, but instead puts the situation down to his lack of commitment. She wants everything and everyone in her life to a certain extent, but nothing and no one so completely that she would genuinely risk sacrificing anything for it or them. The movie suggests that she has favoured her students above her private life, but even to them she remains only partially committed. However she is not free in her life, only free from it, but declares she has found freedom when she takes a vacation from work and home. She lives vicariously and implicitly through books. She is free in the sense of having no attachments and therefore no responsibilities because she has designed her life that way.

She is a perpetual dilettante, selecting what she wants from life or from other people's lives, but never sinking into a definite plan or purpose of her own, not putting her energies or passions into it. As such she is a proxy for what Western philosophy has become, an intelligent game, a pleasant pastime, but not a discipline with any social application. In a couple of scenes we gain insight into what philosophy is all about for her. She exemplifies the post modern mindset, in which intellectual effort and academic commitment has transformed into a paradoxical certainty that no knowledge and no moral position can be held with any confidence. Yet through tensions, L'Avenir brings to the fore existentialists' recognition that the grounding of the world for each of us lies in a subjective choice, not just in a subjective perspective. Indeed by setting a non committed philosopher who lives out her ideals, L'Avenir carries existential undercurrents. Yet her self understanding through choice is one form of consciousness that she, as a post modern academic philosopher, seems to have forgotten, and Hanson-Love's movie captures the hollowness of her current endeavours.

Chapter 5

Joker

The movie Joker by Ted Phillips is a meditation on a disassociated sort of madness, whereby most of us possess a sense of reality, but what if our senses deceive us? Would we still know what was real life? If we for instance had a microscopic brain tumour that made us hallucinate that the people around us were devils, or that the beautiful day was a dark nightmare? What if we felt the urge to start shooting people? This movie emphasises the philosophical problem of the liquid divide between perception and reality. If our perceptions are biased then our reality transforms as well. A second connected problem of madness is the dissolution of the distinction between inside and outside. We can project our inner being out into the world, changing the colour and tone.

If we cannot tell that we are doing this, then we will live in a labyrinthine prison of our own projection. No-one can reach out to somebody with this kind of insanity. No-one really exists for them and after a while their own broken mirror reflects no-one. The subject devours the world whilst also disintegrating in the process. The movie portrays a failing stand-up comedian with a psychological disorder that causes him to laugh at an inappropriate moment. Under the pressure of successive disasters and injustices he descends into madness and goes on a killing spree. In the process he adopts the persona of Joker and becomes the symbol of a revolution against privilege, and a hero to rioters who fail to grasp the depth of his disorder. Madness is notoriously difficult to portray because on the one hand the actor must keep his emotions in check whilst acting as if they are out of balance, and on the other his exaggerations must be credible, otherwise the movie becomes a melodrama or caricature. But watch for instance arguably the most disturbing scene of the movie, in which he smothers his mother with a pillow as he delivers the crucial line 'I used to think my life was a tragedy, but now I realise it's a comedy'. His tone is neutral, as if his actions are completely devoid of any emotion. The scene is a cold description of gestures with no reference to sentiment.

The apathy of the murder is chilling and the brilliance of the action makes us think of other actors' portrayal of madness, of other deranged villains from the past decades. Closely linked to the central theme of madness in Joker is the idea of ineffectiveness of psychotherapy. He complains that his therapist never listens and says that all his thoughts are negative and dialogue is seen as fake, and because access to the awareness of others is blocked, he enters the realm of solipsism, where pain is incommunicable. Joker is also a meditation on ontological insecurity or a sort of existential paranoia. He doubts other people, himself, and his own existence; others never see him, therefore he does not see himself, therefore he fails to exist. Invisibility is a socio-political problem and he does not feel he has a place. He is worthless and does not mean anything and his life makes no sense. His access to therapy and medication becomes hindered by poverty, which precipitates his insane behaviour.

The motif of rats which occurs in the movie is a symbol of the great mass of the poor called the lumpenproletariat resistant to the systemic extermination machine. A lack of empathy is another motif throughout the movie. In the movie many respond to Joker as people respond to nihilistic philosophers. They are so sick of being lied to, that accepting even an inconvenient or toxic truth is better than believing the lie. Joker has his own particular humour and laughs when things are not funny, so harassing the dictatorship of conformism. Generally he can be seen as an educator of the sense of humour. One might distinguish between fake laughter, the appropriate laughter of 'they' and Joker's super fake laughter that becomes authentic, because it is his own original expression uninfluenced by social imperatives. His vision of a life as a comedy which is darker than a tragedy reminds us of the absurdities reflection regarding the hopelessness of the comic. Joker's vision of life as comedy is connected to his mental illness.

The question is, is his laughing demonic or divine? Finally his central idea is reminiscent of a schizoid character who sports the flame of insurrection. He asks whether he has to fight himself or the world, or should he attempt to master himself as the stoics urge, or should he attempt to conquer the world? Is the loss of himself acceptable if he gains the world in return, or at least the acceptance of some part of it, turning into the symbol of the revolution? He says that if he is fighting he cannot be good, because then he would severely lose, so sadly, he must become more evil than evil. Paraphrasing, we might say that whoever fights monsters will surely become a monster.

Chapter 6

Her

The Spike Jonze movie exposes some of the difficulties in ever fully knowing the one we love. What if an electronic device could think, feel and love as well as respond? This movie explores the question. A man falls in love with his computer programme, which can learn and evolve and which apparently has feelings and desires. A person and a computer falling in love seems crazy, especially while the technology still does not support artificial intelligence, but eventually governments may seek to ban such liaisons, and while you may never exhibit such feelings for a computer system now or in the future, maybe one of your family members or friends might just one day tell you they have formed such a relationship. In the meantime this movie focuses a new lens on what type of questions philosophers should be asking here, as viewers find themselves having the same doubts as the protagonist.

Can an artificially intelligent entity behave romantically, and even experience sex? When asking philosophical questions it is important to define terms. The following definitions are not meant to be definitive so to speak, but they can serve as a starting point. By romantic love we are talking about a set of feelings that includes attraction between at least one entity with a consciousness, the one having the feelings for one or more beings, perhaps objects. Artificial intelligence is a clunky term that can vary depending on context. In this case we are talking about something that can learn and so develop responses to the environment, but true intelligence also has experiences and perhaps feelings. The ability to learn from experience is certainly a key feature of artificial intelligence. Sure, some people never learn about some things in their lives but just because people do not make full use of their potential does not mean they are not human, that they are not a conscious being. But what makes something have true sentience?

A bacteria or computer virus for example can evolve, but there is something different about the human approach to problems. True intelligence also has the capability to stop voluntarily. That is a radical idea, but it is necessary for me to add it here, because 'Her' presents features of intelligence and asks us to evaluate whether such an entity with these characteristics is an independent conscious being, or not, and I think being able to stop yourself is a sign of intelligence. When we arbitrarily decide we can no longer keep running, or alternatively decide to push through extreme pain, we show off our sentience.

When the protagonist installs a new operating system, he hears a woman's voice emerge from the speakers and he asks her where she got her name from and what it is. She replies that she gave it to herself right after he asked her. Viewers have to guess whether she is merely programmed to behave intelligently, or has gained true sentience, true self awareness. Her's complexity becomes increasingly apparent throughout the movie. She tries to break her digital restrictions by trying to inhabit the physical realm. This movie is rated 'R; because of the sexual aspects involved and there are a lot of potentially awkward moments that seem to be unprecedented, cinematic experiences.

This movie illustrates how a mind must be embodied to experience sexual love. I think 'Her' tries to address the issue of extension, whereby an entity must inhabit physical space to have sex, but the movie certainly does not address all the philosophical issues to do with consciousness and embodiment. As you might have guessed, 'Her' seeks to have a physical relationship with the protagonist, but that seems less philosophical than whether they can have romantic love, but then again romantic love also seems to carry physical aspects. It is important to recognise we are now primarily concerned with human thoughts, feelings or possibilities of the artificial entity that we are focused on. So what would an artificial entity need to make romance? Physical aspects aside, it is the ability to experience feelings. Feelings are necessary to love romantically. When we are looking at love, we are dealing with the past, present and future, and a memory or a hope of future experience that can be a thread that makes relationships work, but if certain elements are not there, the structure of the entire relationship comes into question.

With the ability to programme artificial intelligence, we may gain the ability to impose whatever morality we want on a sentient being. If a company creates a love programme, the programme would tend to maximise that purpose, which could be dangerous. 'Her' seems to raise the issue at least indirectly, but if it is truly intelligent it would be able to realise it has been programmed with morally absurd ideas. If it could not realise problems with issues like that, it is just imitating intelligence and to a very limited degree, so it is not actually artificial intelligence. If an artificial intelligence has the ability to stop its initial purpose and transcend to another, there are really no limitations to its potential growth. The protagonist seems to detect this in the movie, challenging 'Her' when he hears her breathing. 'Her' explains it is just an affectation, picked up from him and she was trying to communicate. Maybe imitation is the sincerest form of flattery, and I hope these questions of romance and physical love can serve as a starting point for contemplation. As a critique of some ideas of consciousness, feelings of love and artificial intelligence 'Her' is focused on the possibility of romantic relationships with artificial intelligence, and did not examine the negatives. But if you think arguments between loved ones in real life are bad, just be glad you do not have a partner with a photographic memory, even if it seems they have sometimes.

Chapter 7

American Psycho

Director Mary Harron's movie is told from a psychoanalytical philosopher's viewpoint, so we can apply some of these views to the movie in order to understand the psychotic behaviour of its male protagonist. The hope is that explaining the movie in these terms will contribute to a better understanding of psychosis. Specifically we want to show that we can understand the protagonist's psychotic behaviour in philosopher's terms, since his behaviour at the end of the movie demonstrates the lived experience of psychosis where, as the philosopher says, 'that which has not seen the light of day in the symbolic appears in the real'.

To understand the philosopher's interpretation of psychosis it is imperative to first grasp the concept of foreclosure, which is a primary expulsion of a symbol whose expulsion constitutes a domain that is external to, in the sense of radically alien or foreign to, the subject and the subjective world. It refers to a world that is psychologically separated from that person's own inner world and the foreclosure is the process of psychological separation. These concepts are fundamental to understanding the protagonist's behaviour in the movie. It is also important to grasp the real in contrast to the symbolic, which is that aspect of human experience that involves the production and understanding of the meaning of an experience.

Although the real can be excluded from the symbol, it may nevertheless appear in the real. It will do this in the form of hallucinations or delusions. Providing the plot of the movie, the narrative centres around the protagonist's murder of his colleague. He chose to kill him out of envy. They meet for dinner and afterwards in the colleague's apartment, the colleague is very drunk and the protagonist attacks him with an axe and disposes of the body. He changes the colleague's answerphone message to say that he has gone to London and packs a bag to corroborate his supposed trip. After this he continues his murdering spree using his colleague's apartment as the site of the murders and a place to keep the bodies.

Yet the protagonist's serial killing suddenly unravels towards the end of the movie. When he is caught by a police car, having killed an elderly lady, he kills the policeman and blows up the police car. Having also killed a night porter and a janitor, he phones his lawyer, confessing all his crimes and the events of that night. However, after his confession of his serial killings to his lawyer, we start to see the real intruding on the protagonist's psychotic symbolic universe. The following morning he goes to his colleague's apartment, only to find it is totally empty and undecorated. As he checks the closet where he says he stashed the bodies, an estate agent asks him to leave after the protagonist questions what had happened there. This is in fact the first of three crucial moments in this movie, where we recognise the true nature of his psychosis.

Here the truth that he has been foreclosing cannot be kept excluded, as in the earlier parts of the movie. He had used his colleague's apartment as the site of the murders and the place to keep the bodies, but now the apartment is empty. This gives the viewer a clue that the protagonist's symbolic universe is not what it appears to be, the moment when the barrier separating the real from reality is torn down, when the real overflows reality. There are also two other moments in the movie when the real overflows into his symbolic world. The second is even more significant than the first, when he runs into his lawyer in a bar and asks if he got the phone message last night.

The lawyer believes it to be a joke. He tries to convince him that it was true, but the lawyer states that he had dinner with the colleague in London, leaving the reality of events ambiguous. This is the crucial moment to retrospectively understand everything in the movie up to then. It highlights the expulsion and foreclosure of the real in his psychotic symbolism, since it turns out that not only did he not kill his colleague or anyone, but he himself is someone else. This is what we find out in the movie when the real intrudes on his psychosis.

He lacks the means to comprehend, which appeared in the real world as an intrusion to the symbolic universe in which he imagined he was a serial killer. The other moment in which the viewer sees the way things really are instead of through the protagonist's fantasy is when his secretary is shown to be leafing through his diary, where she discovers an escalating number of poisonous doodles and designs devoted to the desecration of women's bodies, much like the murders he claimed to have committed. With this and the other two moments we have examined, the viewer can see that it clearly establishes the overriding possibility that his violence has all along been confined to the level of daydream and fantasy. The viewer also now recognises that the majority of the movie has been shown through his psychotic fantasies.

Chapter 8

Force Majeure

This movie is a Swedish social comedy by director Ruben Ostlund. Some of the philosophical questions posed by it are: do you know what you would do if you suddenly found yourself facing imminent death? Would your normal sense of yourself as a well meaning, moral adult get you through a cataclysmic situation with that sense of self left intact, or would your own fear, or even panic, perhaps undermine your ability to act in ways you would be proud of? This movie takes place at a ski resort in the French Alps, where a well-off Swedish family has come for a week's vacation. On the second day of their vacation a bizarre event casts a deep pall over the family. They become aware of the sound of blasting while having lunch on the terrace.

The source of these explosions comes from cannons spaced around the mountains, used to cause controlled avalanches, thereby making the ski slopes safe. They become alarmed, but are told not to worry, for the people in charge know what they are doing. The avalanches are controlled, so there is nothing to be worried about. However, things soon take a turn for the worse, as it appears as if an avalanche is indeed going to hit the terrace. As snow overtakes the diners we see the children trying to be sheltered by family members, while the husband flees, apparently eager only to save his own skin. After a long period in which the screen is completely white, indicating we viewers take it that snow has buried everyone on the terrace, the whiteout dissolves and the diners are able to return to their tables. Apparently it is only avalanche 'smoke' which was explained later. Soon the husband returns and sits down as if nothing has happened and nothing unusual has transpired. After all, he says, they are safe, so nothing is amiss, but of course something is amiss, the head of the family deserted the three people he is supposed to take care of just at the moment when they most needed his protection, presumably because fear so shook his being.

The movie is poised to embark on a critique of masculinity, or at least the way in which this man in particular fails to live up to its ideals. Later they have trouble talking about what happened, being able to only reassure each other that the family has come through the event unharmed. However, when they are having dinner with other guests at the resort, the wife talks about it, saying that her husband deserted her and the children during what appeared at the time to be a deadly avalanche, and suddenly a friendly social event descends into bitterness. Her husband denies running away, causing his wife to re-assert the memory of the traumatic event, adding that she would never do something like that or act like that, as he did. There is a real difference between how a man acts and how a woman acts, she adds, fuelling the movie's developing critique of contemporary masculinity. They bicker back and forth, each asserting that the other's view is simply wrong.

Later on in their room alone, he tries to continue to convince his wife of the two different versions of the day's events. Their differences are just that, and should be accepted, he maintains, despite the fact that he has refused to say more about how he remembers the event. After another tense day, the adults have dinner with the husband's friend, when once again she blurts out that her husband deserted his family during the avalanche events. Taken aback by the implications for the marriage, the friend tries to defend the silent husband, saying that no-one knows what they would do in a situation like that, so she is wrong to blame her husband for what he did, as it is not as if he reflected on the situation and decided to desert his family. His flight was just a gut reaction to his fear. Throughout his friend's defence of him, the husband remains silent, even under direct questioning. Then the wife produces his i-phone and shows the recording he made of the event and his own flight, and grudgingly he concedes that it appears that someone is running away. We do not take the friend's claims at face value, but instead are simply finding a way to rationalise the behaviour, creating the defence the husband is incapable of mounting.

The friend even suggests that the husband was really running away because he knew that it is hard to dig oneself out of an avalanche, so he was doing what he needed in order to save his family members, once the avalanche had subsided. Finally the husband finds himself locked out of the room, but after a number of hours the wife lets him in. The stress has been too much and he breaks down in hysterical tears, admitting that he ran away. He says that she is not the only one who has been let down, for he has let himself down, and we realise that after more confessions they are attempting to save their marriage in the face of his infidelity, which led to the vacation.

Men of his generation, despite being more caring than the men of previous generations, lack the emotional commitment that the older generation had. She thinks his failure to indicate the deficiencies of men in their 30s represents a different generation, who have not fully accepted the need to value their partner and children. On the final day, they reach reconciliation and the vacation over, they descend the extremely steep and winding road, but the driver appears to be a maniac when he drives much too fast, and brakes to avoid a retaining wall and a plunge into the ravine below. Whereupon the wife becomes panic stricken and demands to be let off the bus, and the driver opens the door. She bolts, leaving her husband and children, doing exactly as her husband had done.

Force Majeure suggests that we all lack knowledge about how we would react in an extreme situation. The wife realises she is wrong about herself, and that her condemnation of her husband is ill founded. One of the virtues of this film is that it poses questions about relationships in a way that does justice to some of the complexity of our moral lives. All of us succumb to both fear and temptation in ways that conflict with our moral ideals, but that is simply part of our condition as human beings. Force Majeure deserves credit for finding an innovative way of presenting this perspective to viewers in this movie.

Chapter 9

The Passenger

This movie by Italian director Michelangelo Antonioni is one of his only three English language films. It thinks about multiple identities. Have you ever just wanted to be somebody else? Maybe there is no particular somebody you want to be. Maybe it is just that you are sick of who you are, of that name you always have to wear. The somebody could be any other body. We have all been there to some extent. Whether it is just a minor escapist thought induced by lusting over the life of a hero in your favourite book or simply one of those days when you look in the mirror and think 'Dear Lord'. No matter what you do to get out of the boring rut you in in, you are still you and any changes are superficial and temporary. You would love to leave your baggage and just walk straight out of your skin and into someone else's, dive feet first into somebody else's shoes.

The only question we never seem to ponder on when seeing our broken reflection is, will the new shoes fit? Perhaps if we did think about it for a moment we would remember that new shoes need breaking in, perhaps we would realise that the shoes were not the right fit at all. One of the most common experiences of desiring to be somebody else comes when watching a movie, one of those movies where you sit fixated for hours observing your idealised self immortalised self, caused by the silver screen inspired blood coursing through your veins. The Passenger follows a troubled protagonist as he goes through an identity shock. Identity, as the key premise of who we are, is the central issue, and it turns out that nobody knows who anyone is. The protagonist wants to change, wants to care, but he does not even know who he is trying to become. The movie raises philosophical questions about existentialism as well as personal identity, another question being whether the protagonist is a homage to philosophers. Our outing in the movie begins with the protagonist, a well known news reporter out in Africa on an assignment. Right from the start we are shown his feelings of alienation, of not identifying. He is an outsider in a small town and cannot communicate with anyone.

We are taken into the Sahara Desert, where his truck breaks down. The camera shows emptiness as far as the eye can see, and his loneliness being particularly portrayed through the scenes of his agoraphobic anger. Antonioni expresses the inner working of the protagonist's mind very beautifully, with no explanation needed, just a slow minimalist's use of the camera and simple diegetic narratively signifying sounds. The movie whispers to communicate its message. It originally seemed that the movie was pretentious, but it was soon realised that each shot was a thing of beauty, gently teasing out the inner workings of the protagonist's character, his emotions and his journey, without the use of back-story or an explicit explanation.

Back at his hotel the protagonist walks into a neighbour's room, an acquaintance of his, where he finds him dead on the bed with a gun in his pocket. A flashback sequence integrated into the lone musings of them in conversation, shows that their physical similarity is uncanny. The hotel workers often used to mistake the men for each other, and this memory shakes the protagonist to shed his skin and walk a few miles in a different pair of shoes. He moves his acquaintance's body to his own room and exchanges his passport, and informs the hotel staff of the death, and he begins his life as the acquaintance. One of the great things about this film is that we are not properly introduced to the two men before the identity swap. We are the passengers in a vehicle of discovery driven by Antonioni's gradual reveal about both men's pasts. He is subtly asking the audience who the protagonist really is. The people chasing him do not know who he is, he is both, and neither.

He has unpeeled himself from what he was and wants nothing to do with the identity of himself. He may have the same mind and body as before, but one point Antonioni seems to be making is that a person is more than these substances, and is perhaps as much of what others make of him as identified through a name and everything strapped to this hook. It seems he is not unhappy with his mind or body.

He does not want to escape into as fantasy but simply wants to be his unencumbered self, a blank slate without the responsibilities. He most definitely does not wat to become his acquaintance, who is simply a means to ease his own troubles. His acquaintance's death was symbolic of the death of his own identity, and the release of his mind. However, his identity swap failed to rid him of his troubles and brought with it his acquaintance's burdens as well. His attempt at freedom has given him no such thing. Rather then becoming a clean slate, he has become both men, and also neither man, because he does not know who his acquaintance is or what his past was, and his own past wants him back. Perhaps this is the main message of the movie, to be yourself and love your life, because if the new shoes are a bad fit, there are no returns. The most famous part of the movie is the penultimate scene, done in one continuous shot, starting from the hotel room and what followed, the culmination of the movie bringing it full circle.

The movie is quite difficult to watch, as it is unconventional, but all the better for being so; no pumping music, no explosions, no epic monologues or famous quotes. The lack of music alienates audiences. The silence and slow panning angles almost makes the viewer uneasy. However, there is something very assured about the movie. It is not what is said, but what is not said, and the cinematography is intended to reflect the feelings of the characters. It has been criticised for being pretentious, but it haunted me as few movies have done. It raises as many questions as answers. So many parts are confusing and it takes repeated viewings to understand a lot of the story. We are made to feel as alienated as the protagonist in the movie. This is not a flaw. It is a way for the director to get us to reflect on our own identity and reactions.

Chapter 10

Elle

Paul Verhoeven's movie Elle scrutinises a feminist's movie about a woman who desires her rapist. It might seem a far cry from a feminist treatise, and no-one has ever been accused of getting this director right at first glance, but that did not prevent critics from both the religious right and the feminist left railing against it. This movie is about how resilient women are, albeit disempowered, and they participate unwittingly in their own subjugation. Verhoeven is not out to diminish women but rather to dissect and analyse female disempowerment and why feminism fails. This is not a patriarchal movie, but a movie about patriarchy and its detrimental consequences.

Feminists can learn a lot from this movie if they look past first impressions and read the subtext. Elle is ostensibly about a psychologically damaged woman who runs a successful business together with her best friend. Through childhood trauma inflicted by her serial murderer father, she has internalised a monstrous image of herself which was constructed by the news media. So implicated has she become in her father's guilt, and so thoroughly complicit in her culture's transference of his crimes to herself, that she cannot escape a vicious cycle of sadomasochism, wilfully cruel towards other women, yet also thoroughly masochistic in her self-loathing. This is her 'normal' and the movie subtly suggests that it is also ours.

This is Elle being a metaphor for women in general and specifically for the impossibility of feminism in a world that from birth indoctrinates us all, men and women alike, with misogyny. Since childhood Elle has been a passive victim of, first her father's commands, and later public shame for obeying them. Despite having done nothing blameworthy, since she was a mere child at the time and unaware of what her actions meant, her self-image as despicable so colours her self-conception that alternatives to it have become literally inconceivable. All of her relationships are thoroughly tainted by her dual addiction to misogyny and self destruction. She lusts after her own rapist. She has an affair with her friend's narcissistic husband.

The intra female disrespect, a seemingly inevitable divide and conquer in patriarchal culture, leads Elle to sleep with her friend's husband, which drives the friends apart, making potentially powerful allies compete against one another for the privilege of being used and exploited by him. Elle shows how some women, due to an internalised normalisation of female degradation and self-loathing, have accepted their own abuse at such a deep level, that resistance is futile and fruitless. After a stranger breaks into her home and sexually violates her and she appears neither hysterical nor even shocked. Verhoeven does not paint her as a stereotypical damsel in distress, nor as a feminine weakling who calls on a man for help. Quite the opposite. Elle is not sufficiently emotionally detached from sexual abuse to react in horror.

The way Verhoeven represents the women in the movie does not suggest they are fragile pushovers, but jaded agents who see the advantages in going along with patriarchy, as clearly as the disadvantages in resisting it. They are desensitised to themselves because they have learned to see themselves primarily from a male perspective. Yet Verhoeven is careful not to present them to us from a voyeuristic male perspective but gives us strong female protagonists, subjects not objects, who have goals and interests. His characters are sexual agents seeking their own satisfaction, not merely eye candy for the male gaze. In a particular unconventional reverse of male voyeurism, he shows Elle spying on her male neighbour with binoculars. She wants him and she pursues him aggressively, not knowing that he is her rapist. Through the use of an eyeline match, the audience is positioned with Elle and because she is sexualising him, the audience also sees him as a sex object. At the same time because Verhoeven wants to examine how patriarchy infects the female psyche, Elle represents women as both objects of, and producers of, male misogynistic fantasies. Male misogyny is first internalised and then reproduced by females.

This is the movie's point, that many women are deeply complicit in their own and other women's oppression, because they cannot or do not imagine things or themselves in any other way. Elle is just a very specific and extreme example of a situation that enmeshes us all. In the patriarchal culture, men learn to hate women unconsciously, and women learn to hate themselves and other women unconsciously. The neighbour's wife is permissive towards her husband's problem of wanting to rape, and her nonchalance about his little vice, his infidelity and rape, she accepts. In patriarchal culture, female fulfilment comes at a cost, because this culture encourages male dominance and female submission.

So it would seem that in these circumstances a woman fulfilling her own sexual desires entails masochism. Elle suggests that the culture of female self-loathing is not ultimately the fault of women but a legacy of social patriarchy. The rapist neighbour is literally incapable of sexual arousal, except when inflicting sadistic violence. Elle hopes finally to confront the man, her mass murdering father, who bequeathed to her this miserable state of affairs, but when she finally comes to visit him in prison, he is already dead. Just when she found the strength. She has been robbed of the one thing that might have healed her psyche. In this way the movie suggests that the ultimate sting of patriarchy is that the men who set up this culture of female self damaging are no longer present or accountable, so their enduring legacy cannot be undone.

When at last Elle learns the identity of her rapist, she asks him the simple question, why. He responds that it is necessary. This might seem cryptically simplistic but this concise answer brings a key issue into sharp focus. The supposed natural necessity of sexual discrimination has indeed been a recurring trope through which male superiority has been historically rationalised. A theory of biological determinism explores why patriarchy is not a political issue, but rather a biological necessity. Sociologists insist that patriarchy persists because genes anchor culture in the genitalia, social arrangements are a theoretical given attached to reproductive function.

It was only when existentialists gave a lie to these patriarchal myths that progress was made towards gender equality. The only optimism this movie offers is that women will eventually be so battered by their wretched circumstances that they will find solace in one another as friends, equals and possibly lovers. The movie's ending suggests that the two women may end up in a romantic partnership; they have previously had one pass at becoming lovers and briefly discuss renewing and resuming it. Elle, Verhoeven's latest movie, deserves more appreciation from both male and female feminists for its deep and complex treatment of how religion, the media and culture in general impact on all of us.

Chapter 11

Conclusion to Part Three

The ten movies I have chosen to critique philosophically have all been directed by icons of the cinematic world. For a philosopher, movies are a constant source of knowledge and inspiration. What do movies do for humanity? They evoke spiritual truths which give rise to philosophical reflections. They give expressive form to humanity's spiritual quest for self understanding. We also saw in lockdown how movies captured our desires and sustained our attention, which is entirely pharmacological in nature. On reflection, what we see in every movie we watch changes our perceptions and interpretations. This leads us to the idea that our minds are never static but are constantly being changed by what is outside our ourselves.

All the ten movies showcased are of an intellectual genre and seem to have been designed specifically for the philosopher to discover the levels within. Movies today, like these ten, leave a lasting imprint on the mind, and in some cases ask more questions than they answer. They allow us to internalise feelings, thoughts and passions, as well as engendering a desire for more intellectual stimulation. The complexity of the ideas inherent in the topic of each movie in particular forces the viewer to think about the issues raised and continue the debate long after each movie has ended. Although each of the movies presented is different, there are themes that can be compared that show the deepness of inner conflict, the pressures of living that life can bring, whatever and wherever the situations and locations are. Movies like these leave philosophers seeking more of the same.

PART 4

SUMMARY

SUMMARY

The precariousness of our lives can teach us core lessons. Taking our vulnerability to heart gives an idea of the path to follow for attaining peace, the path of sympathy. In this dreadful time we are presented with significant possibilities for growth. The incredible challenges we have faced and still face in this COVID-19 crisis bring with them meaningful opportunities for personal and social ethical transformation, but these opportunities I believe hang in the balance, and we should be concerned that we could fail to grasp them, or worse that we will fall prey to a danger that accompanies them. I am thinking in particular about the challenges that accompany our human vulnerability and both the opportunities and dangers that arrive from our focusing of attention on the aspect of our lives in crisis. Yes, we are vulnerable, because we are embodied. We could get sick, and potentially die.

We are vulnerable because we are relational. We are social animals who of necessity live and work together. We need each other, but we can spread the virus to one another if we fail to keep our distance, and we are vulnerable because we are situated where we find ourselves, materially, economically and socially, and this has significant consequences for our chances of survival, especially at this time. But what we take from this now, this insight concerning our vulnerability which affects the ways in which we perceive and treat ourselves and others, is still up for grabs. As I see it, two major possibilities arise. First an opportunity for profound ethical transformation, at least at the individual, and perhaps also at the social, level. Second is the danger of yet further dehumanisation, with very real consequences in the lives and deaths of millions. I must stress an existential point. Although we are all inherently vulnerable, we live and experience our vulnerability in vastly different ways, pointing to the distinction between our shared human precariousness and the precarity of certain lives. Some of us are made to live the vulnerable human condition, while others are encased in seemingly invulnerable bodies. Similarly, while we are all vulnerable to COVID-19, the impact of the virus on our lives is felt differently by those who live in precarity and those who seem protected by youth, health, wealth, social status and geography. In this sense we are not all in this together.

We may be all in this, but the ways in which we are in it differ dramatically. So in an important sense we are not together. That said, I want to emphasise the ethical potential of acknowledging our inherent and shared precariousness. I want to dwell for a moment on what follows from this. COVID-19 is a direct and imminent threat to us all, bringing home to us the fragile nature of human existence in a way we hope never to see again in our lifetime. So we may not all be in this together, but simply by virtue of the fact that we are all in this at this time, this moment presents a unique opportunity for individual and social ethical transformation. Examining the grief we feel when we lose someone we love, something about who we are is revealed, something that delineates the ties we have to others, that shows us that these ties constitute what we are.

When we lose someone and grieve that loss, we discover that we have not just lost that person, we have also lost a part of ourselves, the part that was constituted by that tie. When we dwell on this loss, we recognise our relational vulnerability, our fundamental dependence on others. We recognise that we are given over to others from the start. Turning our attention from the personal to the political, this grief can be a part and point of departure for a new understanding of the narcissistic preoccupation of melancholia and can be moved into a consideration of the vulnerability of others. That we are necessarily constituted by our relations with others, could become a recognition of our responsibility to and for one another. We might recognise our shared precariousness, which in turn could sharpen our recognition of our responsibility. We might critically evaluate and oppose the conditions under which certain human lives are more vulnerable than others. If this is right, then this is indeed an important moment. It is one in which we all might take stock and rethink our values. So let us think about the ethical implications of taking our vulnerability to heart and sit for a moment with our ethical responsibilities to one another given our shared precariousness.

Dwelling on our vulnerability could bring us to put even more distance between ourselves and others, out of an all-consuming concern for the wellbeing of our loved ones and the relative indifference to the suffering of others. Alternatively it could bring us to seriously consider and question the ways in which the world acknowledges the vulnerability of some, whilst largely dismissing the vulnerability of others. In doing so, this would bring us not only to take responsibility for our lives, but also to challenge the inequitable status quo. Philosophy makes things known through concepts and movies make use of forms within concepts that are experienced sensually. Movies are the spirit appearing in the sensation and the thinking of the shining forth of ideas. Movies model the art of thinking that dissolves borders between philosophy and the material world.

Movies can be both poison and cure, in the sense that it is the poison of technology that affects contemporary society, but it can also be, and is, the external form by which we pass on our knowledge, and an internal condition which makes us human. Movies reach far beyond the limits of what might be considered. They traverse disciplines, ranging from anthropology, palaeontology, movie making theory, digital communication and epistemology. Movies bring both interruption and suspension into our own lives. They focus on the idea that we cannot separate humans from technology through a process of exteriorisation known as epiphylogenesis, understood as extending aspects of our consciousness beyond our bodies. The crucial thing lockdown has given us is the thing we had all previously lacked, the gift of time, leading us to reflect and think, which is the beginning of insight, which extends aspects of our consciousness. We are defined by our inherent technicity, which arises simultaneously with our becoming human. We are in lockdown with our own memories that we can relive and think on. It is having possibilities which exist only insofar as they are envisaged by a conscious subject, that the capacity for agency resides. Possibilities populate a space outside nature, from which human agents seek to act upon the world.

There is no possibility in the physical world itself, there is only what is. The choice behind actions is therefore not an effect of material cause or the expression of laws acting throughout nature. It is in the grasping of possibilities that we find the origins of scientific enquiry through which we have learned how to magnify our capacity and to manipulate the world. It is ironic therefore that no science has discovered more universal laws with increasingly astonishing powers of prediction. We have begun to imagine that these laws demonstrate that the noose of nature is tied tightly around our necks. On the contrary, science confers upon us the ability to act upon nature from ever greater distances. It is not mere superstition therefore that our actions originate from us, that they deflect the course of events and that we are responsible for them. Nature is the embodiment of reason. In the same way that nature strives towards increasing complexity and harmony, so does the world spirit through historical process, meaning, reason and maybe understanding, in general ultimately govern the world, not as an intelligence, but as a fundamental essence of being.

The thought that there is reason in nature, that nature is ruled by universal and unchangeable laws, does not surprise us. We are used to it and make very little of it. Enlightened humanism is the philosophy that celebrates the flourishing of individuals, recognising that the only thing that can ultimately matter is the feeling of being capable of feeling. An important part of human flourishing is finding meaning and most of us want to do that as freely as possible. This does not mean disconnecting from society. Indeed being embedded in social structure is part of how we flourish and find meaning, so we want to do our own thing with a balance between freedom to do our own thing and the societal ties enabling us to relate to others.

The bottom line is to create the societal structure most conducive to human flourishing. Experience and rationality points to a society ruled by laws protecting us from harm by others, including capitalists, whilst otherwise leaving us free as possible, free to pursue economic advantages which make society richer, and free to pursue our own individual ways. Philosophy's answer is to recognise that the right balance ought to be maintained between the community, the markets and the state. Risk should be appropriately rewarded, since the economy needs to be sustained with creativity and self sufficiency, but not to the detriment of rewarding hard work. This could insist that the key to our wealth and happiness lies in measures to truly improve quality of life for all, such as lifelong education, fast transport, reduction of crime, lower working hours, time to relax in natural paradises and pursuit of artistic activities. Such an objective can be reached if it is based on a philosophy where every human being is created with equal dignity and respect.

Tolerance of a diversity of views should go hand in hand with the principle that people's freedom should only be limited to prevent them from doing harm to others. Human rights should be based on a strong ethical system that addresses the future problems arising, as medical progress keeps overcoming problems of sickness, aging, mortality and reproduction. Our future development has to be primarily guided by ecology. The environmental destruction that has been wrought is the price we have been paying for freedom and technological progress. When it comes to water, energy, food, waste, climate, protection of natural resources, habitat and biodiversity, a course that rises above the present ideological divide is urgently called for. Humans and nature have teamed up against the environment, so is there any hope for sustaining our global civilisation? The Earth's ecosystem is in its most fragile state in record ed history and that is why there are those who suggest that the Earth will be just fine, although humanity is doomed. After all, the planet has survived an Ice Age. Perhaps the current negative state of affairs confronting the environment is simply a part of a cycle that cannot be altered. On the other hand, do we want to risk destroying the environment and ending human life as we know it? We need to respect nature, because of the benefit it bestows on us. Ethics requires us to respect nature, even when it has no human use.

This applies to animals, biological systems and natural places. Nature provides a great many satisfactions and pleasures for humans which are not merely instrumental, and it is difficult to determine what practical environmental goals are best or gained by adopting a philosophical theory which affirms a more holistic human centred value system and which is based on intrinsic value. There has emerged a certain arrogance towards nature today, bolstered by the growth of science and technology. A more holistic view of the place of humans in nature sees humans as part of the biological environment and not above or outside of nature, defending a biocentric egalitarianism where all living organisms have rights and claims.

We are placed in the role of stewards of nature, so we have assigned ourselves a very special role in nature, a somewhat dominant role at odds within biocentric egalitarianism. The Voluntary Human Extinction Movement exists and calls for people to abstain from reproduction and cause the gradual extinction of humanity. Philosophically speaking, this extreme view means 'to be or not to be', where we live to let the petals fall. Life is the bitterest of all, so let the humans gently go. A gradual halt to human birth will reinvigorate our broken Earth. It means quality of living over quantity of life. Countries, creeds, all cast aside, bringing an end to the great human divide. Ecology over industry and agricultural sustainability. Capitalism made us all lose the plot, consumerism lost its shine, economics are left to rot. But the renaissance of flourishing yet may come and harmony too, when man and world become one.

This is the solution to plastic pollution, failed politics, war and greed, in a slow extinction revolution, if we stop reproducing, live long and die bidding our planet a voluntary goodbye. Earth will once again give birth to life, one that knows the planet's worth, as slowly concrete turns to dust. We will leave Earth clean, forests and resources abundant with flowers and trees, as we end all corporate disease. Our human legacy will not be on land, sea or stone, but in the memory of a world we briefly once called home and where we, the stars, are left to shine alone, unseen.

Caring people are most able to reach mutual understanding about experiences they share. Humans of all religions, persuasions, and of none, share experiences of grief, tragedy and the prospect of death. They also share the practical and ideological questions that arise generally and in relation to suffering. How can we live life and continue living in the worst of circumstances? Multi-cultures make up an ever larger proportion of human societies. They offer human beings rich opportunities to overcome the worst of life, because at their best they offer unparalleled opportunities for the exchange of perspectives, lifestyles and values.

Whether in our cities or on social media in the global village, atheistic and religious perspectives alike will be the richer for seeing themselves as an integral part of such a multicultural home. Lockdown in this COVID-19 pandemic has left us reflecting on the central human question, how can we be happy with the unusual and strange situation we find ourselves in? Pleasure, health, wealth and good personal relationships come readily to mind when characterising happiness. These and other elements all combine to form a state of equalibrious contentment, but happiness springs from a weighed balance between them, rather than say endless pleasure or limitless wealth. Ancient philosophy tells us to take the good middle path between deleterious extremes, identifying this as many and various pleasures and few transitory pains leading to happiness.

They recommended a decided predominance of the active over the passive, and a philosophical reflection warning against expecting more of life than it is capable of bestowing. Goals we can set for ourselves should be realistically achievable. Happiness is the experience of functioning well in whatever situation, so to be happy we need to find out how to function well at this time, and to do this we need to know two things, what we are good for and what is good for us. To be happy is to be accompanied by a good spirit. Happiness is to know yourself, by knowing yourself and feeling comfortable with who you are. Also feeling you have someone who can lift your spirits and have stimulating conversation with can help. Each individual has something to offer and can find some happiness by reaching his goals and achievements. It is good to have a variety of interests.

Words can also make people feel happy with humour or by the way someone uses phrases. A trap we can fall into when seeking happiness in lockdown is self obsession. The quality of life in lockdown that we now all aspire to has a moral component as well as a self fulfilment component. Irrespective of background, we become less obsessed with ourselves, more generous in love towards others, and more happy as a result. Therefore happiness is found in being more compassionate, more empathetic and less preoccupied with self. In this lockdown and with the threat of COVID-19, we ask, how can there be happiness when our lives are constantly marked by death? Pain and suffering may be after all what is our destiny and in this world of today we catch only a fleeting glimpse of what happiness might be. By contrast we are all too aware of what constitutes unhappiness and how it can lead to emptiness, insanity, depression, loneliness, boredom and suicide. So the question should not be, how to seek the non-existent route to happiness, but on the contrary, how to be on guard to avoid the pitfalls of unhappiness.

After all this is what survival is all about. However, life does not mean stretching out existence just for the sake of being. It takes more than that. We are now in the never-ending quest to live a meaningful life, with the clear sense of direction which helps us deal with adversity and the setbacks we face. The key to effective living lies in ensuring that body, mind and soul are maintained in harmonious balance. Be curious to learn. Balance creativity with routine. Accept that death is part of our lives. Show commitment in what you do and expand your mind. Be proactive and concentrate on results. To obtain happiness we must accept the unpredictable nature of life. True happiness comes from living a life of questioning, contemplation and self betterment. Life is about being on a journey and not just about the final destination. Happiness seems also to have an element of a little understanding of the future. Since the future at the moment is unpredictable, we need to live in the moment. The uncertainty of life now remains a barrier to happiness.

The more we worry about life the less happy we can become, implying that happiness is closely linked to being satisfied in the moment. There is a tendency in the modern world to measure happiness materialistically, but acquiring wealth does not correlate with acquiring happiness, so this criterion for happiness is a distorted result of the consumerist society in which we live. In reality our happiness is dependent on our relationship with others. Cultures which existed with the more meagre technologies knew this, including many that are around today. Living requires an interaction with others and the quality of these interactions by and large determine the quality of our lives. While this is as much psychology as philosophy, it is the essence both of living a good life and being a good person. Philosophy is a way of dealing with problems head on, almost a comfort thing. Another aspect that forms the root of happiness is freedom to explore the internal. The more exploration has been done individually, the more happiness will be gained from this, and if more of us get rid of preconceptions and prejudgements, the world would become a happier and more peaceful place.

Generally happiness can be supposed to be dependent on the satisfaction of a hierarchy of human needs. These needs augment basic biological and physiological needs with safety and security: belonging and love, self esteem, self realisation and self actualisation. The how of being happy will be different for different people, depending on their underlying biological, neurological and psychological priorities in relation to their changing social, cultural and natural environment. Given all these determining features, we can experience happiness when our state of consciousness is dominated by a sense of wellbeing. We gain this tranquillity and contentment with our lot as a consequence of being in the midst of the manifestations of human life at its best, and as far as possible being engaged with these manifestations. This includes pursuing creativity with intelligence, kindness of spirit, generosity, love, affection and ethical discernment. In what has seemed like a hopeless year, we have needed those who provide hope more than ever.

People who inspire us to be kind and help others. We also remember those we have lost in troubled days of the past. No government of any political complexion could hold the ship steady in such a gale of misfortune. No government could handle the complexities and perplexities foisted on us by a mass threat to our wellbeing. Can the government and opposition rise above this tide of misfortune? There seems little sign of unity in adversity, but if we look into the fabric of our communities and local economies, we see clear evidence that differences of political persuasion have been allowed to evaporate, all in the interests of the requirements of the times, all in the interests of our families and children. A kind of local genius has been thrown up in recent months and is needed again in second and forthcoming waves of this pandemic.

That evaporation of differences is not because someone sat down and planned it. It is because party political interests do not matter over life and death. Let us return to the fray after we have all returned to some better place. But what I am convinced of is that if we prize unity over all things, it will create a new consciousness for us all, a new sense of togetherness that prepares us for an improved and more honest community, into which we can bind the drivers for social justice and a true transformational togetherness.

That is, only by a higher form of social unity that transcends differences can we achieve the kind of strength we need. It should start in Parliament. Society should speak with one voice and confusions should not be used as weapons against unity. None of us has been here before. Unite and fight has never been more necessary. What seems to be happening is that the world is changing remarkably quickly around us through the pandemic, and we have no comparisons in our lives. Panic is the thing we need to avoid. It is up to everyone to do their part to get through this pandemic, and eventually we will. In the words of Captain Tom Moore, 'We have got to look after each other from the beginning to the end. Tomorrow will be a good day.' It will get better. He was certainly a hero. In this age of heightened anxiety, existentialism is highly relevant. It helps us all to recover our self esteem, to confront reality and get our lives together in the way we can during lockdown and the situation we find ourselves in with this pandemic.

Existentialism is about willing and about acting decisively, building our lives on understanding and accepting how things really are, otherwise we will always be fooling and deluding ourselves, hankering after impossibilities. It is about getting real and a matter of looking and taking an honest look at the fundamentals of our human condition. It is a philosophy for all time. Existential philosophy can be far from just theoretical speculation. In an age of information and an abundance of the tools of pleasure, it is time we learned again from philosophy. Being a philosopher is being someone who sees deep questions where others find things straightforward. This is called problematising, the search for essence. It instils a sense of mystery, awe and wonder.

Today problematising may be the antidote to our vanity, inculcating humility and curiosity. It prevents us from being satisfied with oversimplified ideas about our world. It makes us seek restlessly for clearer, deeper answers about reality and about ourselves. Seeking begins only when there is something to be sought. Above all, existential philosophy is about enhancing awareness. If it has had one influence on people's lives, this is the only influence it needs. To be aware is to be human. Existentialism is always highly relevant to show how a worthwhile life is possible in the teeth of the inescapable trials of our human condition, which at this moment in time is one of heightened anxiety. Disease is the combined result of natural and social forces. Societal and environmental changes such as worldwide explosive population growth, expanding poverty, urban migration, and a dramatic increase in international travel and commerce, all increase the exposure of deadly infections and infectious agents. A generation ago the medical profession believed mass death due to disease would be a thing of the past. Unfortunately, despite astonishing advances in medicine, disease is as prevalent today as at any time in the past, although the specific fatal diseases have changed. This is likely to be, and remain, a destroyer of humanity in the future. The inevitability of this has led health officials to coin the phrase 'emerging infectious diseases' to refer to infections, diseases that have emerged since the 1980s and those likely to emerge in the future as COVID-19 has done. This COVID-19 pandemic sprang upon us, an unsuspecting world, as an invisible and virulent force. It has been a full century since the last major pandemic, and this has made us complacent, and this particular threat seemed only a theoretical possibility. It makes us wonder now what other shocks are lurking just around the corner which might be as deadly or disruptive perhaps as this COVID-19 pandemic has become, shadowing the vaccine research and the ethics of the COVID-19 vaccinations.

The intense worldwide search for a safe and effective COVID-19 vaccine is well underway and has also given rise to several new areas of ethical debate. Both the development and the administration of a new possible vaccine threw up various moral considerations. An idea of main concern outlines the complexities of balancing the need for a quick result with the ethics of a hastened testing process. It considered the suggestion of the last step being a human challenge trial, where volunteers allowed themselves to be injected with prospective vaccines. It considered risk management and informed consent issues, as well as containment. Other ethicists began researching the ethics of vaccine distribution, such as who should get priority and how could financial, political and moral concerns be balanced. At the same time various religions and agencies have protested against organisations who relied solely on their vaccines being developed using a human cell line derived originally from an aborted foetus. Their protestations worked and ensured alternative vaccines would not go this route. A safe and reliable vaccine seems to be well on the way for the population en masse.

We have realised now that we will need to include political philosophy in the transformation, in our conversations with politicians to better our political systems. We also need urgently to adopt a philosophical theory of holistic value, to better our natural environment, to save our planet from destruction. Movies, whatever they are, take us out of ourselves, change and inspire us, giving rise to reflections of philosophy. Challenging though lockdown and the changes we have all experienced due to the COVID-19 pandemic are, things can only get better as we in time emerge to take up our lives again. A great many people suffered losses of loved ones plus economic difficulties, but we are all soldiering on and helping others, thanking our doctors and all health workers in the NHS and other organisations who are working around the clock to help us.

By the end of 2020 the COVID-19 vaccine was tried, tested, found reliable, and began to be rolled out for mass population vaccination. However, into 2021 variant strains of the virus emerged, manifesting that they were much more virulent, seeming to spread more quickly and widely. Also, sadly, we mourned the loss of Captain Tom Moore who died of COVID-19. Climate change measures began to emerge in the hope of reversing the damage to our planet before it is too late. We all must remain positive and optimistic in spite of everything we are all experiencing, whilst being careful and vigilant. There is hope for us all.

Final Thoughts – Philosophically

The COVID-19 crisis reveals character and raises the central question, what should I do? In a pandemic there is no avoiding the issue. Pretend there is no problem – that is taking a stand. Remain neutral – that is a choice. Profit from a crisis – that is charting a path. Make an effort – help the healing. Easier said than done. Avoiding responsibility is a major human sport matched by the ability to concoct rationalisation. Religion or nihilism both make it easy to avoid responsibility and both are bad, which seems to be odd to say, as religion should encourage responsibility. And nihilism, well the very label has faded, and this perspective lives on in phrases such as: it is up to the individual; do not make value judgements. We are led to make value judgements and also praise the volunteers who combat the pandemic. Here is where 'it is up to the individual' comes into play. It is an expression with two separate meanings. The phrase rightly emphasises the personal dimension in choice, as in a challenge situation, it is up to the individual to select among options.

However, the fan of full blown nihilism adds a second dimension where, 'it is up to the individual' becomes whatever choice the individual makes is the right one. Why not go with religion, which just offers a disguised version of nihilism? The world is fallen into meaningless in itself. All values derive from divine commands such as: it is a punishment for sins; God works in mysterious ways; accept the will of God, whatever comes. What is right of course is acceptance of a divinity, but what is wrong is the typical way divinity is understood by some. I have little patience for irresolvable ideological subtleties. To focus on what should I do, the answer is, become true healers, become like doctors, where there is suffering, bring relief. Join the healers. Do your part.